T0258328

# Death and the Ploughman

**Johannes von Saaz**

Translated by

**Michael West**

**Methuen Drama**

Published by Methuen Drama

1 3 5 7 9 10 8 6 4 2

First published in 2002 by
Methuen Publishing Limited

A CIP catalogue record is available from the British Library.

ISBN 0 413 77303 5

Typeset by SX Composing DTP, Rayleigh, Essex
Printed and bound in Great Britain by
Cox & Wyman Ltd, Reading, Berkshire

Gate Theatre presents

# DEATH AND
# THE PLOUGHMAN

by **Johannes von Saaz**

Translated from the Middle High German
by **Michael West**

First performed in Britain at the Gate Theatre, London,
on 28th October 2002, as part of **A Politick Death**
season, Autumn 2002.

# DEATH AND THE PLOUGHMAN

## by **Johannes von Saaz**

Translated from the original Middle High German
by **Michael West**

| | |
|---|---|
| **Death** | Madeleine Bowyer |
| **Death** | Tim Barlow |
| **Ploughman** | Simon Meacock |
| **Death** | Ben Nealson |
| | |
| **Director** | Deborah Bruce |
| **Designer** | Imogen Cloet |
| **Sound Designer** | Jason Barnes |
| | |
| **Assistant Director** | Selena Kelly |
| **Stage Manager** | Elizabeth Dudley |
| **Technical Assistants** | SJ. Anthony & Jacqualine Eckel |
| | |
| **Costume Assistant** | Sarbs Chopra |

## For the Gate Theatre

| | |
|---|---|
| Artistic Director | Erica Whyman |
| Producer | Kester Thompson |
| General Manager | Daisy Heath |
| Associate Director | Kate Wild |
| Production Manager | Neil Sutcliffe |
| Technical Manager | James Glanville |
| Education Officer | Herta Queirazza |
| Box Office | Paul Long |
| Trainee Directors | Vicky Jones & |
| | Richard Twyman |
| Researcher | Martine Dennewald |

**Thanks to our volunteers:** David Linton, Cherie Huang, Anna Haustein, Nick Foltz, Vicky Lane and to all our volunteer crew, who often work long and unsociable hours in order that this theatre may survive.

Gate Theatre,
11 Pembridge Road,
London
W11 3HQ

| | |
|---|---|
| Box Office: | 020 7229 0706 |
| Administration: | 020 7229 5387 |
| Fax: | 020 7221 6055 |
| E-mail: | gate@gatetheatre.freeserve.co.uk |

**Tim Barlow**          Death
Tim was in the army for fifteen years before becoming an actor. Trained at Bristol Old Vic.
Joined Théâtre de Complicité as an associate artist in 1985, for **More Bigger Sacks Now**. Complicité directed and produced his one man show **My Army** (world tour). More recently played both **King Lear** (Sheffield Crucible), and the Fool (Bristol Old Vic).
Recent TV includes: **Night and Day, Mile High, The Bill.**
Recent Film includes: **Les Misérables, Rocket Post.**

**Jason Barnes**          Sound Designer
Jason trained at the Bristol Old Vic Theatre School and is now resident Sound Engineer for the Bristol Old Vic. Sound engineering credits including: **Love off the Shelf, Wizard of Oz** and **The Surprise Party** (Nuffield Theatre, Southampton), **Nymph Errant** (Chichester Festival Theatre), **Blues Brother Soul Sisters** and **A Streetcar Named Desire** (Bristol Old Vic).
Sound Design credits include: **The Surprise Party** and **Earth and Sky** (Nuffield Theatre and UK tour), **The King of Prussia** and **Insignificance** (Chichester Festival Theatre). Whilst at the Bristol Old Vic he has designed sound for **Bitter With a Twist, A Busy Day** (Bristol and West End), **Denial, Croak Croak Croak, King Lear, A Bitter Herb, Look Back in Anger, One Love** (Bristol and Lyric Theatre Hammersmith), **Up the Feeder, Down the Mouth and Back Again, The Real Thing** (Bristol and UK tour), **Molly Sweeney, Antigone, The Beggar's Opera, A Chorus of Disapproval** and most recently **Mrs Warren's Profession.**

**Madeleine Bowyer**    Death
Theatre includes: **The Garden of Delights** (National

Theatre Outdoor Season), **Moby Dick** (with Kaboodle / Walk the Plank), **On the Boil** (Prithvi Bombay), **The Breakfast Soldiers** (Contact Theatre Manchester) **Twelfth Night** (Bridewell),**Our Day Out** (Sheffield Crucible), **Sheherezade** (Forest Forge), **The Woman Who Swallowed a Pin** (Hammerton Hall), and **Pygmalion** (Tour de Force).
Television includes: **Emmerdale, Harry and Cosh**, and **Primal**.
Film includes: **People Like Other People, Amen ICA Cinema**.


**Deborah Bruce**        Director
Deborah was the Resident Director at Theatr Clwyd where she directed **The Glass Menagerie, My Sister in this House, Hello and Goodbye, Our Country's Good** and **Oleanna**. Recent credits include: **Behsharam** (Birmingham Rep and Soho Theatre), **In Praise of Love** (UK tour), **Made of Stone** (Royal Court), **The Woman Who Swallowed a Pin** (Southwark Playhouse), **The Asylum Project** (Riverside Project), **Making Noise Quietly** (Whitehall Theatre and Oxford Stage Company tour), **Written Off: 4 Prison Plays** (Almeida), **Romeo and Juliet** (Chester Gateway), and **The Inheritor** (Royal National Theatre Studio).


**Imogen Cloet**        Designer
Imogen trained at the University of Hull.
Recent theatre credits include: **Noir, V, You'll Have Had Your Hole** (Northern Stage), **The Last Post, Bones, Cooking with Elvis** (Live Theatre), **The Selfish Giant** (Leicester Haymarket), **Le Chat Noir** (Theatre Sans Frontieres Tour), **The Ghost of Federico Garcia Lorca** (Foolsyard Theatre Co. Tour).
Film credits include: **Flickerman and the Ivory Skinned**

**Woman**, **Bait**, **Psyche Out**, **Inbetween**.
Exhibitions include: **Popolo** (Gusto, Newcastle), **Puce**
(Playhouse Gallery), **Triptych** (with Bernadetje), and
**March** (Bread and Puppet Theatre).
Imogen has been nominated for the Barclays TMA best
designer award 2002 for her work on **Noir**, and is the
sixth Jerwood Young Designer at the Gate.

**Selena Kelly**          Assistant Director
Selena is currently training at Central School of Speech
and Drama.
Theatre credits include: **In High Germany** (Lion and the
Unicorn), **The Bower Wall** and the Galway Youth Theatre's
**More Light** and **Taking Breath** (Nuns Island Theatre,
Galway) and assisting on **Sweeny Todd** (Central).

**Simon Meacock**          Ploughman
Simon trained at the Central School of Speech and
Drama.
Theatre includes: **The Robbers** (Gate), **Our Country's
Good** (Theatr Clwyd), **Peter Pan** (West Yorkshire
Playhouse), **Comedy of Errors** (RSC and world tour),
**Benchmark** (New End Theatre) **Macbeth** (West End).
TV includes: **Menace, Killer Net, Casualty, The Bill,
The Crooked Man, A Touch of Frost**.
Film includes: **Joan of Arc, Sorted, If Only**.

**Ben Nealon**          Death
Ben trained at Drama Centre.
Theatre includes: **Harvest** (Southwark Playhouse),
**Search and Destroy** (New End Theatre), **Twelfth Night**,
**The Importance Of Being Earnest** (Colchester Mercury
Theatre), **Passport To Pimlico** (Tour), **The Signalman**
(Windsor Theatre Royal).
TV includes: **Soldier Soldier, Bugs, The Bill**.

Film includes: Patrick Smith in the Oscar nominated **Lagaan.**

**Michael West**          Translator
Michael has most recently adapted **Lolita** for the Peacock Theatre and The Corn Exchange. For the Corn Exchange he has also written **Foley** (Traverse and Hampstead Theatres) and **A Play on Two Chairs**, he co-devised **Car Show** (Observer's Top 10 theatre events 2000), and wrote a translation of **The Seagull**. In collaboration with **Team** he has written two plays for children, **Forest Man** and **Jack Fell Down**. Other original plays include **Monkey, Snow**, and **The Death of Naturalism** (for radio). He has also written versions of **The Marriage of Figaro** (Abbey Theatre), **Tartuffe** (Gate Theatre, Dublin), and for Pigsback, Molière's **Don Juan**, and **The Tender Trap** (after La Double Inconstance by Marivaux). He is currently under commission to write **The Evidence of Things** for the Abbey Theatre. **Death and the Ploughman** was originally commissioned by Project Arts Centre in a co-production with La Comédie de Reims.

# Revelations – The Gate Translation Award

The discovery of hidden riches in international drama has always been at the heart of the Gate's work. To highlight the vital role translators play in this endeavour, we re-launched our Translation Award in October 2001, under the title Revelations.

The response was staggering. The 73 entries submitted were of a very high quality and included many plays which have never been produced in this country. Six of the most intriguing and accomplished translations were selected for our shortlist. These were then judged by an independent panel of judges. **Death and the Ploughman** was deemed to be the runner-up.

The Gate now intends to establish the Translation Award as a regular biennial event and we look forward to celebrating the skill and significance of the best in translated work in future years.

We would like to thank all the translators and playwrights who submitted entries, and all the sponsors who have made the award possible – especially Oberon Books and Jenny Hall. We would also like to thank the panel of judges: Jack Bradley, Dominic Cooke, Jo Ingham, Katherine Mendelsohn, Meredith Oakes, and Nicholas Wright.

**The other short-listed texts were:**


**Witness** by Cecilia Parkert,
translated from the Swedish by Kevin Halliwell
(the winning entry)

**Massacre** by Bergljót Arnadóttir,
translated from the Swedish by Gabriella Berggren

**Nirvana** by Konstantin Iliev,
translated from the Bulgarian by Anna Karabinska

**Trio To The End Of Time** by Lars Norén,
translated by from the Swedish by Kevin Halliwell

**Sincerely Yours** by Pierre Marivaux,
translated from the French by Steve Larkin

**The Gate's work is supported by**:
The Jerwood Foundation, The Arts Council of England,
Charles Glanville, Jenny Hall, The Paul Hamlyn
Foundation, London Arts.

**Gatekeepers:**
Sir Ronald and Lady Cohen, Jenny Hall, Hart Brothers,
Oberon Books, Georgia Oetker, The Really Useful Group
Ltd, The Really Useful Foundation, and Mr and Mrs Tack.

**Special thanks to the following for all their help and
support on this production:** Simon Cox, Selenz, Paul
and all the staff at The Prince Albert Pub, all the
palantypists who helped Tim, Tracey Elliston and Jack
Bradley.

JERWOOD
FOUNDATION
CHARITABLE FOUNDATION

## young british designers at the gate

*The Jerwood Young Designers at the Gate is a scheme designed to encourage, support and nurture the very best of British theatre design. The Gate has a reputation for the ingenuity and quality of its theatre design, and this scheme builds on that achievement. The Jerwood Charitable Foundation is dedicated to imaginative and responsible funding of the arts and education.*

*As well as the Jerwood Young Designers at the Gate, the Charitable Foundation supports the Jerwood Painting Prize, the Jerwood Applied Arts Prize and the Jerwood Choreography Awards, and has the benefit of association with the capital projects of its parent Foundation, including the Jerwood Space in Southwark, the Jerwood Theatres at the Royal Court and the Jerwood Gallery at the Natural History Museum.*

*The Gate is pleased to announce that all three Gate shows in the Politick Death season, will be supported by the Jerwood Young Designers at the Gate scheme, and would like to thank the Jerwood Charitable Foundation for its continued support.*

**Johannes von Saaz: a note on the author**

The author of *Death and the Ploughman* was probably born in
the village of Schüttwa (Sitbor), in the district of
Bischofsteinitz, in northern Sudentenland. His date of birth
is unknown, but evidence suggests between 1342 and 1350.
Around this time there was an outbreak of the bubonic
plague – the Black Death – which ravaged Europe, killing a
third of the population.

In the documents that have come down to us, the name
of the poet varies: it appears as Johannes von Tepl,
Johannes Hanslini von Sitbor, Johannes von Sitbor or
Johannes von Saaz. Between 1358 and 1368 he was
educated at the monastery in Tepl, after which he studied at
the University of Prague, and finally in a university in either
France or Italy (Paris, Bologna or Padua) where he acquired
the title Magister Artium.

Having finished his studies, he worked for a period in the
Imperial Court at Prague. In 1378 Johannes von Tepl was
appointed municipal notary (*notarius civitatis*) to the town of
Saaz and in 1383 he became headmaster of the school
there; he held both positions until 1411.

In this year he left Saaz for Prague where he became
clerk and he died there in 1414. Few of his other writings
survive: some verse in Latin and three volumes of
administrative and juridical papers which he drew up in his
capacity as notary and legal counsel in Saaz and Prague.

On 1 August 1400 his wife Margherita died in childbirth.
This painful episode inspired the creation of his masterpiece
*Death and the Ploughman*.

**From a letter by the author addressed to Master Peter Rothirsch, citizen of Prague, accompanying the text of** *Death and the Ploughman.*

The love which united us in childhood, in youth and the fullness of age, prompts and obliges me to console you and to make a gift of that which you asked of me through M. de S. – a product of the field of letters where it pleases me to glean after having missed the harvest. It follows that I send you this poorly constructed, vulgar work in German, fresh from the anvil. But in view of the seriousness of the subject which I gave myself (consisting of an attack against the inevitability of death), one finds therein all the elements of style. Here a major theme is briefly treated, there a minor one is expounded; the piece consists sometimes of praise, at others of blame, and often both side by side. The exact expression jostles the inexact; often you will find the same word for different things, or different words for the same thing. There are groups of words and phrases in the current style; occasionally they appear alone, sometimes in extended sequences. Irony casts her bitter smile, figures of speech and tropes abound. Other trifles, both acceptable and disallowed in this inflexible idiom, show themselves in all their glory; I hope that they will find indulgent ears . . .

**Translator's Note**

For most of the time theatre is a blunt instrument of the
entertainment industry; this is true for even the most
dedicated practitioner or devotee and it is what makes a
play such a depressing mixture of dread and hope. Yet
occasionally the elements conspire to make it relevant, and
to everyone's surprise there is an eruption of something
primal on to the stage.

   This is one of the foundation myths of theatre – it is
central to the art form's appeal as a redemptive act – and it
was in just such language that I first heard of this strange
and beautiful six-hundred-year-old text.

   Christian Schiaretti, now the artistic director of the
Théâtre National Populaire in Lyon, worked for a time in a
small studio in Paris. While there, a German colleague of
his, Dieter Welke, introduced him to *Der Ackermann und der
Tod* with the suggestion that he think about mounting a
production. He thought about it and they set about
translating it into French.

   *Der Ackermann und der Tod* is not, as it may appear, an
obscure relic, a deep-sea-dweller brought to the surface of
modernity like a mangled coelacanth. Called variously the
first German text of the Renaissance, or the last of the
Middle Ages, it is prescribed as a school text in Germany. It
has a life as a folkloric document, a medieval lament in a
voice as distant as Chaucer, utterly unrelieved by bawdy.
People have heard of it in Prague and Vienna. You can buy
it in several editions accompanied by a modern German
version. I used the excellent pocket-sized Philipp Reclam
Jun. (Stuttgart) edition with a translation and notes by Felix
Genzmer.

   No, what is most remarkable – although this may prove
wild speculation on my part – is that its availability has
acted as a sort of shield, and that while it was taken up with
delight by nineteenth century German scholars this seminal
text of modern Western thought waited almost six hundred
years for translation into a neighbouring language.

   Of course there are certain reasons for its silence. For one thing it is not, strictly speaking, a play. But as a personal testament and historical record, it offers a unique insight into a period of European civilization that is frequently dismissed as the Dark Ages. It contains within its argument the foundations of the Reformation; it is the anguished cry of an individual facing up to the abstractions of God and religion. It is certainly one of the most blasphemous articles of piety in Western literature.

In any case, Schiaretti's production first appeared in 1989 and toured Eastern Europe as the Berlin Wall came down. It had a profound impact on those who witnessed it, and on those who made it. When I came to know him, Schiaretti had become the artistic director of La Comédie de Reims, and *Le Laboureur de Bohème* (the lovely title of the work in French) had become his signature piece. Its name was uttered in hushed tones by misty-eyed people of all persuasions. It had become a mythic beast: the perfect piece of theatre, and now it lay preserved in the aspic of nostalgia, never to be disturbed.

So it was with some surprise that in the autumn of 1999 I was introduced to a theatre producer in Dublin as the translator of the play into English. Surprise followed by delight, (for who wouldn't want to tackle something approaching the status of legend?), followed by dread for who would want to tackle something approaching the status of legend and ruin it? Besides, how on earth would you approach such a task?

I began with Schiaretti and Welke's French version which left me in a state of cold panic. There was no clue how to proceed in English, there was no foothold in the language. Christian said I should meet with Dieter Welke and look at the original text in German, so we met up in France in the summer of 2000, and we began. I remember vividly the first time I set eyes on *Der Ackermann und der Tod*; I remember vividly the first word. It is 'Grimmiger'. I remember it because when we sat down to read it, Dieter began repeating it over and over, followed by a twenty minute disquisition on history, politics, etymology, law, theology, culminating in a story about flying a plane over the rainforests of Latin America. I think we did about five lines that day.

Anyone familiar with the sado-masochistic pleasures of dense textual exegesis knows how it goes. But even though many nuances of this text must be irretrievably lost to us, this gradual unravelling allowed me to acclimatize to the sound of the language and to encounter the exquisite temper of Johannes von Saaz – or von Tepl as he sometimes appears. There are endless bifurcations in one's dealings with Death.

It has been a rare privilege to work on such a remarkable piece of writing and it is a great pleasure to know that the Ploughman will get to make his prayer once more in a completely different setting.

As a French actor memorably described it, the final speech is like flying an aeroplane in a starlit sky as the fuselage falls away from you, and as each piece falls to earth the flight gets quieter and quieter until finally you are being propelled through space without support, the wind whistling silently through your hair. As I said, this was a memorable description, and possibly the most frightening piece of encouragement I've ever received.

Michael West, Dublin
September 2002

Know now that God hath overthrown me, and hath
compassed me with his net. Behold, I cry out of wrong, but I
am not heard: I cry aloud, but there is no judgement. He
hath fenced up my way that I cannot pass, and he hath set
darkness in my paths. He hath stripped me of my glory, and
taken the crown from my head. He hath destroyed me on
every side, and I am gone: and mine hope hath he removed
like a tree.

(Job XIX 6-10)

To every thing there is a season, and a time to every
purpose under the heaven: A time to be born, and a time to
die; a time to plant, and a time to pluck up that which is
planted. A time to kill, and a time to heal; a time to break
down, and a time to build up. A time to weep, and a time to
laugh; a time to mourn, and a time to dance. A time to cast
away stones, and a time to gather stones together. A time to
embrace, and a time to refrain from embracing. A time to
get, and a time to lose; a time to keep and a time to cast
away. A time to rend, and a time to sew; a time to keep
silence, and a time to speak. A time to love, and a time to
hate; a time of war, and a time of peace.

(Ecclesiastes III 1-8)

## Johannes von Saaz: A Chronology

| | |
|---|---|
| 1338 | Beginning of Hundred Years War. |
| c. 1340 | England: birth of Chaucer. |
| c. 1345 | **Probable birth of Johannes von Saaz (between 1342-1350).** |
| 1347 | Foundation of the University of Prague. |
| 1347-52 | The Black Death devastates Europe, killing one third of its population. |
| 1355 | Charles I of Bohemia becomes Charles IV, Emperor of the Holy Roman Empire. |
| 1368-137? | **Education of Johannes von Saaz at the University of Prague, and universities in France or Italy.** |
| 1360-99 | England: various versions of *Piers Plowman*. |
| 1374 | Italy: death of Petrarch. |
| 1375 | Italy: death of Boccaccio. |
| 1377 | England: death of Edward III; coronation of Richard II. |
| 1378 | Death of Charles IV. He is succeeded as Emperor by his son Wenceslaus IV. |
| | The Great Schism begins with the election of rival French and Italian Popes (Clement VII and Urban VI). |
| 1378-1411 | **Johannes lives and works in Saaz.** |
| 1384 | England: death of John Wyclife, first translator of Bible into English, reformist theologian and opponent of Papacy. |
| 1387 | England: *The Canterbury Tales*. |
| 1388 | Revolt of Bohemian nobles against royal authority. |
| 1394 | Wenceslaus IV cedes power to an assembly of nobles. |
| 1399 | England: abdication of Richard II, coronation of Henry IV. |
| 1400 | **Death in childbirth of Margherita, wife of Johannes.** |
| | England: death of Chaucer. |
| 1401 | *Death and the Ploughman* **written.** |

| | |
|---|---|
| 1402 | Jan Hus (reformer and translator of Wyclife) made rector of University of Prague. |
| 1411 | Jan Hus excommunicated. Prague condemned by Rome. |
| 1413 | England: death of Henry IV, succeeded by Henry V. |
| 1414 | **Johannes von Saaz dies in Prague.** |
| 1415 | Jan Hus burnt at the stake. Battle of Agincourt. |
| 1417 | End of Great Schism. |
| 1420 | Start of the Hussite Wars. |
| 1429-31 | France: Joan of Arc fights the English. |
| 1431 | France: birth of François Villon. |
| 1453 | End of Hundred Years War. |
| 1456 | Gütenburg Bible printed. |

# Death and the Ploughman

This translation was first performed 10 July 2001 at Project Arts Centre, Dublin. The cast was as follows:

**Death**        Lalor Roddy
**Ploughman**    Owen Roe
**Angel**        Clara Simpson

*Directed by* Christian Schiaretti
*Designed by* Renaud de Fontainieu
*Lighting by* Julia Grand
*Costumes by* Agostino Cavalca

**Acknowledgements**
To Christian Schiaretti who led me to water and to Dieter Welke who led me to drink. Thanks also to La Comédie de Reims, Project Arts Centre, the Arts Council/An Chomhairle Ealaion and the Corn Exchange. And finally to the Gate Theatre for their pursuit and embrace.

## PLOUGHMAN (Chapter One)

Butcher most wrathful of all creatures; killer most terrible of all peoples; vengeful destroyer of flesh, Death, be thou cursed.

May God your creator hate you; may monstrous tragedy pursue you; may unending misfortune hunt you down; may shame be your eternal companion.

May fear, distress and lamentations follow you wherever you go. May sorrow and grief accompany you for all time.

May the heavens, the earth, the sun, the moon, the stars of the firmament, the seas, the waters of the earth, the mountains and valleys, the meadows, the dark abysm of hell, all that lives, every living thing be your dread enemy and curse you for evermore.

May you sink into a pit of malice, in pitiful sorrow may you drown. May God banish you from His sight; may you be furthest from His eyes, and from the eyes of all men and ' all creation for evermore.

O evil corrupt! May your vile remembrance endure until the end of time. May horror and fear cleave to you whither you go, wherever you dwell.

Let the truth of my plaint ring out, let my clenched fists bear witness to my agony. O Death, for myself and for all mankind, I seek justice.


## DEATH (Chapter Two)

List, list; listen and marvel; these cruel charges against us, these accusations, whence do they come? Truly, it is passing strange.

Yet threats, curses and hand-wringing demands have never hurt us before.

So, my son, whosoever you be, show yourself, speak forth. What wrong have we done you? Why do you charge us so foolishly?

We have swept many who were learned, noble, fair, mighty, upright, over the edge of the meadow of life; also the widow and the orphan. Many lands, many peoples have had their due lot of sufferings.

They are all silent.

You appear in earnest; we see that distress burdens you greatly. But your plaint is without reason; it rings hollow like the clangour of brass.

If rage and fury speak through you, if you are benumbed and dull with grief, stay yourself; don't be so quick to curse.

Don't fool yourself that you could even so much as touch the cloak of our magnificence.

Unstop your lips. Tell us your name. Tell us how we have wronged you.

We wish to appear just before you; our cause is just. We know not of what you so wantonly accuse us.


**PLOUGHMAN** (Chapter Three)

I am a labourer of the field; the plough is my pen, my nib the ploughshare. I am of the land of Bohemia.

Hatred, malice and contempt must I evermore bear to thee. For you have taken from me the twelfth letter of my alphabet; you have torn the flower of my delight from the meadows of my heart. You have stolen from me what can never be recovered.

It is right that I am angry at you, that I press my suit against you. By your hand I am cut off from the sweet hours of my life, from the country of joy.

My days were not long enough, my nights were too short with her.

And now I am told: 'It is done. Begone.'

Dark clouds oppress me, I am withered and barren, I lament without cease.

I am driven before the wind, cast adrift on the savage sea. The waves have the upper hand. My anchor is torn from its moorings.

And so I will cry without end: 'Cursed be thou, O Death; Death, be thou cursed.'

**DEATH** (Chapter Four)

This outburst astonishes us; we have not met its like before.

If you are a labourer, and of the land of Bohemia, we think you do us great wrong; for a long time now we have done nothing in Bohemia.

Save for recently, in a pretty fortified town, set fast on the side of a mountain.

There we did our work of grace with a young woman of virtue. Her letter was the twelfth; she was perfect and upright, and she walked with God.

We were there when she was born.

And when the Queen of Honour bestowed on her a crown and cloak of velvet, leafed in gold. She bore it to the grave, intact, immaculate, and whole.

Pure of conscience, she was good and faithful, and without blemish in the eyes of the Lord. She was gentle and constant; in truth we say to you, such a woman comes rarely into our hands.

It is she that you speak of. We can think of no other.


**PLOUGHMAN** (Chapter Five)

Yes, Milord Death. I was her lover, she my beloved.

You took her, she is gone. My shield of peace, my charm against evil; she is gone from me.

And I am alone, a poor labourer of the fields.

My star is plucked from the firmament. The sun of my salvation is set and will nevermore rise; never again will my star of the morning rise before me. Darkest night is everywhere before my eyes.

May eternal agony and woe without end be your lot and inheritance. May you founder in wretchedness.

Vice drips from your teeth, your lips slaver with malice; yet still you are greedy for more.

Death, may you die, may you fester in hell. May God strip you of power, and reduce it to dust. May He crush you underfoot.

**DEATH** (Chapter Six)

A fox smote a sleeping hound, now he will ever run for his life. A hare struck out at a wolf, that is why the hare must course with no tail. A mouse scratched at a cat while she slept, and wonders why the cat is his bitter enemy. And you want to meddle with us. You overreach yourself.

We will prove that the scales are just, that our judgement is just, and just is the way we proceed in this world.

We are like the sun, which shines on good and evil alike. Both good and evil alike must yield to our power.

Witches raise spirits, but cannot deny us their own in the end; neither magicians nor sorcerers, there is none to resist us. Let them sit astride their brooms, let them straddle their goats! Their trappings serve them nothing.

Doctors eke out the span of life; yet they too owe theirs to us in the end. Roots, herbs, ointments, all the apothecary powders in the world cannot save them.

If we were to make known to crickets and butterflies the shortness of their days, no answer would satisfy them.

Should we then spare man, because he takes offence?

The vastness of the globe is ours. All kings will cede their crowns to us; they will put their sceptres in our hands. The Pope with his mitre and crook, his flesh is in our power.

Leave off your cursing. Do not bore me with your market chatter. Do not hit against the rafters lest the dust fall in your eyes.

**PLOUGHMAN** (Chapter Seven)

I curse you, abuse you, revile you. May worse than evil befall you, you will have deserved it.

After great suffering must come great lamentation. I would not be human did I not weep for this gift of God.

I will mourn her for all my days. My falcon has flown; nevermore will she rest on my arm.

I grieve for she was of noble birth, rich in honour, fair, lively; she was paramount among women; loving of truth, prudent in her words, pure and chaste of body, gracious with others, easy in her way of going.

I will refrain my mouth for I am too weak to sing all her virtues which God Himself showered upon her.

This you know full well, Milord Death. Truly, if there was an ounce of goodness in you, you would take pity on me.

**DEATH** (Chapter Eight)

God grants the seat of heaven to the pure of heart, the abyss of hell to the wicked; but dominion of the earth is given over to us.

In heaven, peace and the reward of virtue; in hell, torment and the punishment of sins.

But the four corners of the earth, the waters of the earth, and all they contain: He who reigns over all gave them to us, and bade us tear out the surfeit.

Reflect for a moment, in your vanity and folly; delve in the poor soil of your reason and you will uncover the truth: if, since the first man was expressed out of clay, if we had not harvested men from the earth, animals from the wastes and wilds, fish from the waters of the deep, the very air would be thick with flies, and none could withstand them. None would dare abroad for fear of wolves.

One man would eat another, an animal his brother, each living creature would feed off each living thing because there would not be food for them all. The bounds of the earth would be too constrained.

Fool, who weeps for mortals, desist. The living to the living, the dead to the dead. You would do better to bewail your stupidity than the loss of your wife.

**PLOUGHMAN** (Chapter Nine)

I have lost my most precious treasure, I must wait till the
end of my days deprived of all joy; should I not grieve?

May merciful God, Lord Almighty, avenge me on you
who bring me such sorrow.

You have deprived me of all pleasure, you have taken
from me the days of my life that I counted dear.

Great honour and blessings had I while the daughter of
angels played with her children.

She is dead.

O Almighty Prince of Heaven! How blessed the man to
have married such an immaculate woman.

Though I have known heartache and suffering, I give
thanks to You my God, that I knew this most perfect of
women.

And you, wicked Death, bitter enemy of man, I pray that
God bear you eternal hatred.

**DEATH** (Chapter Ten)

You have not drunk of the fountain of wisdom. This much is
clear from your words.

You have seen nothing of the workings of nature; you
have understood nothing of the way things grow out of each
other; you know nothing of how the world works by
transformation and decay; you are but an ignorant whelp.

Look about you: the gentle rose, the sweet-smelling lily of
the valley, the life-giving herbs, the healing plants, the
flowers which give pleasure in the meadows. Look at the
stones in the fields, the trees soaring in the copses; behold
the bears and the lions in the wilderness; the horses, valiant
and proud; the men, forever skilful, surprising, wise.

Behold all these creatures of the earth. How intelligent
they are! How beautiful! How strong! How alive!

They will all die.

All the generations of men, those that have been, that will

be, no matter how long they live, how long they strive, they will all die. None will escape us.

'This too will pass', should be the words in the mouth of every living man.

Your argument does not hold. Your plaint will avail you nothing. It is the bastard child of your impoverished senses.


**PLOUGHMAN** (Chapter Eleven)

I place my trust in God, who has power over me, who has power over you; I have full faith in Him, He will keep me from harm. He will avenge me for your crimes and punish you for your wrongdoing.

You sing me a song of falsehood, you mix the true with the untrue; you wish to drive the ache from my senses, the pain from my heart, the suffering from my soul.

You will never achieve it; for this loss chafes me greatly, it pierces me through; this hurt will nevermore be made whole.

She was my medicine, my all-healing ointment. God-fearing, obeisant, both day and night she watched over me. She honoured my body with her body. That which was asked of her, she did freely, and often more than was asked.

Merciful God, who will reward the faithful, Lord God Most High, grant her grace, more than even I wish for her.

O brazen assassin! O evil incarnate! May your judge be a hangman, and may he rack you till you cry out: 'Forgive me!'


**DEATH** (Chapter Twelve)

If you truly knew how to measure and weigh, to count and to tally, your poor troubled head would never spout such folly.

You curse and demand vengeance, without wit or necessity. What use is such braying?

Did we not tell you: all who are rich in thought, honour, courage, art, all that has life must die by our hand.

And still you whine and say that all your happiness you found in this woman.

If all happiness is found in woman, then may you rest down beside her; only look to it that out of the bosom of happiness does not spring forth misery.

The more you are loved, the greater your sorrow.

If you knew not love, you would now know less pain.

If you had spared yourself love, you would have spared yourself affliction.

Women, children, all the treasures of the earth, each must bring a small portion of joy at their beginning, the full portion of sorrow at their end.

Suffering is the end of love, the end of joy is sorrow. After pleasure comes the loss of pleasure. All living things hasten to this end.

It is time you learned this lesson, put something of substance into your rattled head.

**PLOUGHMAN** (Chapter Thirteen)

After the blow comes mocking laughter. Thus are the disconsolate treated.

You have taken from me the taste of love, and given me the taste of grief. If it be God's will, then I must suffer it.

As dull-witted as I am, as little wisdom as I have of my betters, I know that you robbed me of honour, you are the thief of my happiness, you have stolen the good from my days.

Wherefore should I give thanks? Where shall I find comfort? Where my refuge? Where shall be healing? Where receive counsel?

Gone. Gone. All my joys swept away before their time.

Who will recompense me my loss?

What are you, Milord Death, that you break all marriage vows and profane marriages?

This kindness you render us, these acts of grace you do unto us, the favours you bestow; may He who has power over the living and the dead make you take them back.

Prince of Heaven, make good this great loss. Avenge me against evil, against Death, Lord God, King of Justice.

**DEATH** (Chapter Fourteen)

Idle words profit a man nothing.

After foolish talk comes discord; after discord, enmity; after enmity, the feud; after the feud, wounds; after wounds, suffering; after suffering, repentance. Thus it goes with the ignorant.

You propose to argue with us. You complain that we have done you wrong in taking your dearly beloved wife.

We were kind and showed mercy.

We have done our work of grace while she was yet young and happy; while her body was still proud and firm, we took her.

All the sages, all the prophets praised us when they said: 'Better to die in the midst of life.' He has lived too long who wants to die.

At the birth of her child, we have let her take leave of this brief life, this vale of tears; we have let her come unto her rightful place with God in the life everlasting, according to His holy law.

And even as much as you hate us, we wish for your souls to be united in heaven above; your body, here, with hers, in the tomb.

This is our solemn vow.

Now stop up your mouth. Be silent. You can no more take from the sun its light, the moon its coldness, the fire its heat, the water its wetness, as take from us our power.

**PLOUGHMAN** (Chapter Fifteen)

The guilty need cover their shame with fine words.

You offer the sweet with the bitter, balm together with torment. Thus do you show yourself before those you wish to betray.

No matter how beguiling your speech, I still miss my wife.

And it is not God who causes me such pain, for if I had sinned against God, which, alas, I have often done, He would have punished me, or she who is without fault would have redeemed me.

It is you the wrongdoer. And that is why I would sore like to know who you are. Who art thou? What art thou? What is thine form? Whence cometh thou? Whyfore art thou?

Why have you torn up the meadow of my delight? Why have you cast down the lofty tower of my strength?

Lord, in all Your creation there is nothing more terrible, nothing more hideous, nothing more unjust, nothing more bitter than Death. Death condemns to despair and misrule Your earthly domain.

That which is pestilent, old, sick and worthless Death leaves behind; the good and the highly prized Death takes away.

Pass judgement, O Lord, judge Thou this false judge.

**DEATH** (Chapter Sixteen)

That which is wicked appeareth good, and that which is good is called wicked.

You accuse us of judging you wrongly, but it is you who judge wrongly; this we will prove.

You ask who we are.

We are the hand of God. We are the reaper who metes out justice. Our scythe cuts its swathe – white, black, red, brown, green, blue, yellow; all the bright flowers, and the grass before us, we reap. We care not for their outward show, their vigour, their innocence.

Its fine colour cannot help the cornflower; neither its sweet perfume nor the sweetness of its nectar can help it.

See you not this? That is justice!

You ask what we are.

We are nothing, and yet are we something. We are nothing because we possess neither life, nor being, nor form. We are not a spirit; neither are we visible nor tangible. Yet are we something because we are the end of life, the end of being.

We are the fate of all men. Titans must fall down before us. All that which has life must be transformed by us.

You ask what form we possess.

We have none. We cannot be enjoined, nor can we be called forth. And yet we have seen our image, in Rome, in a temple, painted on a wall.

There is a man sitting astride an ox, whose eyes have been bound. This man holds in his right hand an axe, and in his left hand, a spade.

With these he is fighting off a great crowd, a multitude, all armed. They raise their hands against him, they cast stones against him, there is even a nun with her psalter.

This mob contends against him, astride the ox, who is an image of Death, who is a picture of us.

And Death buried them all.

You ask whence we came.

We come from the Garden of Eden. God called us forth when He said, 'In the day thou shalt eat of this fruit, thou shalt surely die.'

You ask whyfore we appear.

We have just told you we bring more good than harm on this earth. You should give thanks to us. Rejoice that we look so kindly upon you.


**PLOUGHMAN** (Chapter Seventeen)

The liar dares to bear false witness when it is unknown whereof he speaks. A man who has travelled far and wide, who brings tidings of foreign lands and strange marvels; his lies go unpunished before the ignorant.

You say you come to earth through the garden of paradise, and aspire to justice as a reaper. You say your scythe cuts down all in its path.

Yet your scythe cuts the flower, and spares the thistle. You pass over the wicked man, and take the good.

Show me them now, point them out to me; where are the good, the upright, the worthy who once walked on this earth?

You have taken them, and my love is with them. All that remain are ashes and dust.

Where are they now who lived on this earth and walked with God, who won His grace, His favour and His forgiveness? Where are they now, who were seated on this earth, who could read the movement of the stars and the paths of the planets? Where are they now, those brave, intelligent, just and diligent men of whom the chronicles speak so well?

You killed them all. And my gentle friend also. And the wicked still abound.

Who is guilty in all this? You claim to know truth, Milord Death; you should name yourself.

You pretend your judgement is just, that you spare no one, that your blade cuts them all, one after another.

I was there, I saw with my own eyes two vast armies, who fought in the green meadow. They were wading up to their ankles in blood; and I saw you there, I saw you among them, I saw you everywhere, busy to the end.

Some you killed outright; others you spared. More knights than footsoldiers saw I lying there, dead.

You chose from among them like from a basket of ripe pears.

Is this how you reap? Is this how you judge? Is this how your scythe looks kindly upon us?

Come, children, come. Let us mount on our horses, let us ride to our fate. Let us lift up our voices in praise to this Death, great lord of justice.

**DEATH** (Chapter Eighteen)

That of which you know nothing you should pass over in silence.

We too should now be still.

We have known you a long time. But we had forgotten you were such an excellent man.

We were there when King Solomon on his deathbed bequeathed you his wisdom; when God gave you all the power He allowed Moses in Egypt; when you took a lion by its paws, and hurled it against a wall, we were there.

We saw you count the stars in the sky, and the grains of sand in the sea; we saw you reckon all the fish in the sea, and tally up the drops of rain. We watched with pleasure your famous race against the hare.

When you led the armies of Alexander, and carried aloft the banner under which the known world lay conquered, we looked on and were happy for you and your glory.

At Athens when you held forth with the best of the Academy, when you spoke like an angel on God and man; while they were rapt with attention, we were content.

And while you counselled the Emperor Nero to be patient, we listened on with sympathy.

We were amazed when you led Caesar across the Rubicon, admired your audacity with Hannibal and the elephants.

In your workshop we looked on with wonder as you stitched a garment of rainbows. And on this robe, you sewed angels and birds, animals and fish, and all the creeping things of the earth. Not forgetting the hem, to which you added an owl and a monkey.

Above all we witnessed and we sang to your glory when you were at Troy and counselled first Hector, then Achilles; and when God Himself summoned you to His presence to discuss the implications of the sin of Eve, we deferred to your wisdom.

Had we only known you earlier, we could have followed your teachings; we would have let your wife live, and not

just your wife, but all those who died, all those now
rotted.

And we would have sounded your glory, your glory alone,
for truly, you are an intelligent ass.


**PLOUGHMAN** (Chapter Nineteen)

He who loves truth is rewarded with ridicule.

You credit me with impossible marvels and wondrous
works, you allow me magical powers. You use me ill, it
pains my heart. Contumely, scorn and hatred you pour on
me.

Whether you have acted towards me with justice or not,
I have submitted, I have suffered your hand; have suffered
it and have not sought revenge as I should, in law, have
done.

If I have wronged you in some way, or done something
forbidden, enlighten me, I will willingly make reparation.

But if it is not the case, recompense me yourself; instruct
me how I can lessen the pain in my heart. Either make good
my sorrow, the grief you have bestowed on me, the malice
inflicted upon me and my children; or come with me before
God, our rightful judge, and let Him decide.

I place my trust in you; I believe you capable of justice,
and will recompense me after so great a wrong.

Do this, else the hammer will fall on the anvil. The hard
will fall on the hard. A great reckoning is coming, the day of
last judgement.


**DEATH** (Chapter Twenty)

Kind words calm the multitude; insight restrains them.

A man in the grip of anger cannot arrive at the truth.

If you knew it not before, know it now: from the moment
a man is born, he drinks from a cup that is not his; he must
die.

The beginning is sister to the end; he who is sent out is honour bound to return; that which is suffered by all, must not be contested by the few; that which a man borrows he must restore.

Man lives in this world as a stranger in a strange land. The days of man run with swift feet; he lives and dies in the blink of an eye; death is his inheritance.

And if you weep over the youth of your wife, you are wrong. From the moment you enter this world, you are old enough to leave it.

Perhaps you think that old age is a blessing. Old age is helpless, it is tiresome, misshapen, cold and displeasing to all. It is good for nothing.

If you lament the beauty of your wife, you are as a child.

The beauty of all flesh is taken by old age or death. All the pretty young mouths will wrinkle and fade; all the rose-red cheeks will pale, all the bright eyes become dim.

Weep not for a loss which can never be made whole.

**PLOUGHMAN** (Chapter Twenty-One)

Love the rod of chastisement; kiss the wounds of instruction. So say the Scriptures.

Where there is fair reproach, there also is good counsel; counsel me then, I humbly entreat you.

Free my heart of its pain, my soul of its torment; relieve my mind of its heavy burden.

How to replace so pure a mother for my children? Counsel me, that I be not angry for evermore, and my children be not sad for all time.

Be not full of wrath, for I have seen even the beasts of the field grieve over the death of a mate; it is part of the order of things.

You owe me succour and counsel and recompense, for you have done me wrong. And if you do nothing, then God in His glory will have no dominion. There must be vengeance; once more must fall the axe and the spade.

**DEATH** (Chapter Twenty-Two)

Nyack nyack nyack goes the duck disturbed in her nest; the mongrel will howl for the loss of his bone.

We have told you that the death of all mortals cannot be haggled over like a cheap bolt of cloth. Death is not a kingdom you can choose not to enter. We are the toll gate; we are the customs. At our feet all must empty their lives; through us all men must pass.

Why do you set yourself against us?

Without us there would be no life; without us there would be no order to the world.

Either your pain is too great, or you are losing your senses.

If you are losing your senses, then pray to God and beg of Him wisdom.

If your pain is too great, then desist, abandon your suit, accept that the life of man on this earth is but a breath of wind.

You ask for counsel: how to relieve your heart of its pain.

Aristotle taught that joy, sorrow, fear and hope bring suffering to all.

After joy comes despair; after love, suffering. That is how things must be on this earth.

Suffering and joy are entwined. The end of one is the beginning of the other.

He who does not banish love from his heart will know only sorrow. The moment you tear out all traces of love, all memory of desire, your mourning will cease. As soon as you forget that which is lost, away flees your grief.

If you refuse there is only sorrow before you. It will follow your children far and wide and into their grave; unto your death will sorrow pursue you.

You wish for the mother of your children to be replaced? Can you undo the years that have gone, can you recall all spoken words, can you restore the maidenhood to a woman confined? Only then you can return to your children their mother.

Now have I given you sufficient counsel. Do you yet understand, clumsy fool?

**PLOUGHMAN** (Chapter Twenty-Three)]

With time comes truth. Something learned slowly is a thing learned for ever. Your words are sweet and uplifting. I feel their effect.

And yet, if love and its pleasures were to be banished from this world, the world would be a poor place.

You try to instruct me with examples taken from antiquity; I will do so in turn. Take the Romans.

They honoured and taught their children to honour the pleasures of the body; that one must play, run, wrestle and nurture the physical arts lest one fall into the ways of sloth and wickedness.

Nor the soul nor the senses should remain idle. They are forever contending between good and evil. Even in sleep should they not be idle lest they run to wickedness.

If you were to drive out of the soul its good thoughts, bad thoughts would take their place. The good leave by one door, the bad enter another. Should I deprive my soul of its memories of true love, bad memories would take their place. Thus will I think on my true love for all time.

When a great love is transformed into great heartache, who could forget it so quickly? That is the way of the wicked.

True friends think on each other always. Long journeys, long years apart will never divide them.

And if her body is dead to me, yet her memory lives in me for ever.

Milord Death, counsel me, but counsel me true, else you are but a bat, a foul creature of night.


**DEATH** (Chapter Twenty-Four)

Joy, but not a surfeit of joy; grief, but not surfeit of grief; this is the way of the wise man. You do not likewise.

He who demands counsel yet heeds it not cannot be counselled.

And yet we wish to bring the truth out into the light. Listen who will.

Your feeble powers of reason, the small compass of your senses, wish to make of man something more than he is.

This you cannot do.

That which he is I will relate to you, by leave of all gentle women.

Man is conceived in sin, fed in the body of the mother with unclean and feculent matter. He cometh out of his mother's womb naked but for a cloak of slime. From then on he is but a midden heap of putrefaction, a mewling latrine, a meal for the worms. He is a pestilent wind, a festering pond, a walking carrion, a dancing corpse; he is a mildewed casket, a gamebag full of holes, a bellows, a gaping maw; an overflowing chamberpot, a pitcher of foul-smelling piss, a stinking bucket, a charnel house, an insatiable trough, a painted shade.

Recognise the truth of this. Each perfectly created man has nine holes in his body, and from these holes ooze unspeakable filth.

If you had the eye of a hawk, and could see through flesh, you would tremble in horror.

Go, lift the skirts of the most beautiful woman in the world; you will find a shameless wench; a flower which wilts under the first rays of the sun; a brief shining light that winks out before its time; a lump of clay that comes apart under the first shower of rain.

Show me, show me a fistful of the beauty of these comely women who lived long ago, cup it in your hands; if you succeed, I will give you the Emperor's crown.

Let your love flow, let flow your suffering, let flow the Rhine, the way of all waters, O wise king of the donkeys.


**PLOUGHMAN** (Chapter Twenty-Five)

You air-corrupting, stinking, carcass breath!

When you dishonour the nobility of man, most beloved creation of God, you insult God Himself.

Now I understand your wicked lies; you were not born of paradise, as you proudly claim. Were you truly born of paradise you would know that God set man as the first of all things, the paragon of animals; He granted him power over all and made all things under his foot; He made him master of all the animals of the earth, the birds of the sky, the fish in the sea, the fruits of the earth.

If man were as despicable, wicked, impure as you claim, then you accuse our Maker of a botched and parti-coloured work.

Milord Death, you insult the noblest work of God.

Man is the fittest portion of His handiwork, sublime and free, and made in His own image. Where is the craftsman who has turned a piece as fine, as delicate, as full of wisdom as the head of man?

In its small globe are encompassed round miraculous faculties, the equal of God's wondrous craft.

The bright sphere of the eye, polished like unto a mirror, the vivid witness which can penetrate the skies.

The ears which bring report of far events; perfectly formed, dressed in softest skin, set for the discernment of all melodious sounds.

The nose, whereby the scent-bearing air enters and leaves, for sense of smell, the delicacy of the palate, the enjoyment of sweet odours and delicious tastes.

In the mouth, the teeth, which daily grind the body's food; and there the tongue, that dextrous hinge, which opens to us the minds of others, which also are a kind of sustenance.

And in the head, the thoughts, which animate the soul; infinite in speed and range, man's conceit can reach the bounds of the known universe, can reach even unto God, and yet beyond.

Man alone is blessed with reason, this precious prize of God. Man alone is blessed with a form so comely that only God could have made its like.

Milord Death, you are the enemy of man, and that is why you speak nothing but evil of him.

**DEATH** (Chapter Twenty-Six)

Stuffed full of curses, insults, petty dreams, you are still nothing but a bag of wind. Against a blabbing, prattling fool, words are small use.

I allow that man possesses knowledge, beauty, dignity. I allow it. Yet he will be caught in our net, trapped in our snares.

Grammar, the foundation of all discourse, will avail you nothing for all its overweening certainty.

Rhetoric, the fertile ground of flattery, will avail you nothing for all its flowery terms and delicately shaded argument.

Logic, which teases out the true from the false, will avail you nothing with its deceit, its sly twistings of meaning.

Geometry, which surveys the earth, will avail you nothing for all its faultless measurements, its careful calculations.

Arithmetic, which creates order, will avail you nothing with its enumerations, its agile figures.

Astronomy, the mastery of the stars, will avail you nothing, for all its sidereal power and the influence of the planets.

Music, which brings harmony to the voice, will avail you nothing for all its melody and song.

Philosophy, field of wisdom, path to God, pasture of nature and ethics; it will avail you nothing, for all the perfection of its fruits.

Nor physic, with its potions to soothe the sick; nor alchemy, which transforms base metal into gold; nor geomancy, which finds in the celestial vault answers to the questions here below; nor pyromancy, which sees visions dancing in the flames; nor hydromancy, the clairvoyant study of turbulent waters.

Astrology, the interpretation of earthly events by unearthly signs; palmistry, teller of fortunes in the lines of the hand; necromancy, the occult mistress of spirits; the Cabbala, its delicate wrought prayers and powerful incantations; augury, which can understand the language of birds, haruspicy, the smoke from the altar; pedomancy,

which reads the future in the entrails of children;
ornimancy, in the bowels of barnyard chickens; the lawyer,
the Christian without a conscience, with his sinuous twisting
of the just with the unjust.

This art, and all other arts, will avail you nothing.

Each man must fall before us and be trampled underfoot;
each will be cut down and flayed by our hand.

Know this as truth, insolent farmhand.


## PLOUGHMAN (Chapter Twenty-Seven)

One must not meet evil with evil. Virtue asks of man to be
patient. I will follow this path.

If truth abides in you, counsel me true. How shall I now
live my life? Whither should I turn? Should I remain a man
of the world, or become a monk?

In my mind's eye I called before me the lives of other
men. I appraised them all, weighed them with care; I found
them all imperfect, weak, full of sin.

I am sore wracked by doubt. All ways to me seem pitiful.
Milord Death, counsel me. I have great need of counsel.

In my heart I know full well, a woman so pure and
pleasing to God will nevermore return.

But if He should keep her to Him in heaven, what will I
do here below? I swear by my soul that if the Lord saw fit to
bestow on me another helpmate, I would honour her for the
rest of my days. Lord God Most High; fountain of all
blessings; honour be to those whom You grace with a
companion and bedmate. They should lift their eyes to the
heavens, give thanks to You each day. Do what is just,
Milord Death, most wise.


## DEATH (Chapter Twenty-Eight)

Praise without end, contempt without reason. In praise, as
in insult, one must have measure and balance.

You laud over the measure the state of holy matrimony. We have something to say on holy matrimony.

From the moment a man takes a wife, both are bound in our prison.

Each man drags behind him a dead weight, a ball and chain, a sledge without runners, a yoke, a harness, a side of beef, a wild cat in a sack, to whom he is bound by the law until we show unto him mercy.

A husband is married to thunder and hail; each day in his own home he finds a snake in his bed.

Every day his wife plots against him. Should he wish to rise up, she will drag him down. If he wishes for this, she wishes for that. Should he will to go here, she wants to go there; such games will weary him daily, bouts without end, without hope of winning.

She can scheme, flatter, deceive, caress; she can grumble, laugh, or cry; all these she can do in the blink of an eye, from the day of her birth.

Sick in the day when work is at hand; healthy at night when there is lewdness. Wise or savage, she can be either, according to taste. She does not need enticement to start a fight.

Not to do what is bid of her; to do what is forbidden; this is her way always.

This dish is too sweet, this one too salty. There is too much of this; that is too small a portion. Now is too early, now is too late; thus she rails against him from sunrise to sunset.

And that which she praises, suffer it to pass under the plane, and in the shavings that fall you will find sniggers of mocking laughter.

There is no middle way for a man trapped in marriage; he is either too gentle or too severe, and with either he is wrong.

Each day brings more insolence and bickering; each week, rebellion and grousing; each month brings yet more horrors; each year, daily squabbles and new dresses.

That is the life of a married man.

Of late-night disputes we say nothing; our sense of decorum prevents us.

And we speak only of virtuous women; of the others we could say even more.

You should know whereof you praise. You could not tell gold from lead.


**PLOUGHMAN** (Chapter Twenty-Nine)

He who besmirches the honour of women, besmirches his own.

What is happening to you, Milord Death? Your unprovoked insults to womankind, even where merited, bring shame on you, and to women, dishonour.

Many a wise thinker has said: 'Without a woman at the helm, the man will be lost.' I have never seen a man who is full of courage but is guided by the counsel of women.

It is seen every day where nobles gather, in the marketplace, at court, at tournaments, in battle. When a woman of virtue upbraids with a finger, she punishes a valiant man more than do arms.

In sum, all that keeps us, guides us, enriches us, we owe to women.

Yet beside gold, there is lead; beside wheat there lies chaff; among honest money, there is found counterfeit; and where there are women, so too are there sins.

But the good should not have to pay for the wicked. This you must accept, dread lord of the mountains.


**DEATH** (Chapter Thirty)

A lump of coal for a ball of gold; a piece of horn for a topaz; a bit of gravel for a ruby; these confound the fool.

To take a haybarn for a fortress, the Danube for the sea, a buzzard for a falcon; this is the mark of the dullard.

You praise what you desire but do not reflect on this. Do

you not know that to be in this world is to succumb to the lusts of the flesh, the covetousness of the eyes, or the vanity of the soul?

If you could but see it, you would find vanity everywhere you look, and whether you are attended by joy or sorrow, you would bear it with good grace, and leave us in peace.

But as much as a donkey knows how to play the lyre, so do you grasp the truth.

And that is why we fret for you.

And we who have separated the young Pyramus from his Thisbe, who were one flesh, one soul; who have relieved Alexander of his power over the whole world; who have crushed Paris of Troy, and fair Helen of Greece; none has reproached us as you have.

Though many lament for Aristotle and Avicenna, none accused us as you do. Mighty King David and Solomon the Wise are both dead; and still we are more honoured than cursed.

Those who have been are now gone. You, and all those here with you, all those yet to come, all will follow them hence. For here on this earth, we, Death, remain lord.


**PLOUGHMAN** (Chapter Thirty-One)

A man will be hanged by his own words. The more so when he keeps changing his argument and perjures himself.

You have said what you are, and what you are not; you have said you are not a spirit, you have said you are the end of life. You say that it is to your hands that all men on this earth are entrusted.

You say we must all depart this life, and you, Milord Death, remain master on earth; two conflicting arguments cannot both be true at the same time.

If we must all depart this life, and all earthly life must have its end, and if as you say you are the end of life, then it follows thus: without life there can be no end to life; without an end to life there can be no death.

And what becomes of you then, my good lord?

You cannot abide in heaven, for heaven belongs to the souls of the good; and, in your own words, you have no soul.

If you can do no more on earth, the earth has no more need of you; you should go straight to hell, and there suffer torment without end.

Thus will the living and the dead be avenged. For none can trust in your subtil words of everchanging argument.

Can all that dwells on earth, all earthly creation be so wicked, wretched, corrupt? That is to blaspheme our Maker.

Since the beginning of time God has loved virtue, has cast from Him wickedness. He has forgiven our trespasses, or He has punished them; and so will He do in time to come.

Your argument totters on foundations of sand, and you wish that I abandon my suit?

I call before you to God, my saviour, Milord Death, most corrupt.

May God, author of justice, grant you a wicked amen.


**DEATH** (Chapter Thirty-Two)

It is often the case when a man learns to talk he forgets how to listen.

We told you, we keep telling you, and we wish to have done telling you; it is the earth and all that is in it which is built on foundations of sand.

Since the time of Creation, all suffers mutability; each thing must be transformed. That which is hindmost comes to the fore. That which was at the front falls behind. That which was low is raised up. That which was on high is brought down unto the valley. Good becomes evil, and evil turns into good in the souls of men.

Into the fire's eternal flame I have pushed all humankind.

It is easier to catch a ray of light than to find a faithful friend.

Men tend more to wickedness than good. And if they do good it is from fear of us.

All men, in all their actions, are full of vanity. Their bodies, their women, their children, their honour, their goods, all will pass in the flickering of an eye, in a gust of wind.

Neither sunlight nor shadow will perdure.

Behold and mark the children of man, what yet they do to your beloved earth; how they ravage the mountains and valleys, the fields and the stones, the forests, the meadows, the wooded lands and the wilderness, the bottom of the sea, the depths of the earth; they ransack them all for the love of worldly goods.

Neither rain, wind, thunder, snow, nor all manner of foul weather will stop them.

See how they sink shafts in the ground, bore tunnels, engrave chasms; how they pierce the veins of the earth to seek out precious stones.

They strip the forests of their timber, and multiply like rabbits in the roots; they plant, they graft trees in the orchards, plough in the fields, train vines, divert rivers, raise tithes on the poor, fish and hunt more than they eat.

How many servants they have, how proud they ride on their horses. Behold the chests filled with silver and gold, precious stones and rich clothing. See how they gorge themselves on the pleasures of the flesh; lewdness they pursue tirelessly, both night and day.

What is all this but vanity? A sickness of the soul, as fleet as the day that has passed.

By war and by theft are their spoils won; the more they have, the more they stole; and that they leave behind to sow argument and discord.

The heart of man is set in fear, sorrow, suffering, trouble, terror, pain, sickness, mourning, cries, disputation, screams and other offences against dignity. And the more earthly goods a man has, the more offensive he becomes.

The truth of it all is this: man can know neither the hour nor the place we will appear to him. We will fall on him without warning, and we will send him the way of all flesh.

This burden must be carried by both master and servant,

man and woman; it will be shared equally between the rich
and the poor, the good and the wicked, the young and the
old.

O sorry fate! How little you know!

When it is too late, you try to be good. Vanity of vanities!

Stop your complaint. Whatever your station you will find
only weakness and vanity.

Turn thou away from what is wicked, do what is good;
seek out peace, and hold it dear above all things; love your
clear conscience.

We give our counsel in good faith; we will come with you
before Almighty God, the Everlasting, King of kings.


## ARGUMENT OF THE PRINCE OF HEAVEN
(Chapter Thirty-Three)

### The Judgement of God the Almighty

Spring, summer, autumn, and winter, the four great
guardians of the year, found themselves in bitter dispute.

Each vaunted his abilities, each attempted to outdo the
others by rain, by winds, by thunder and tempest, all the
elements within his power, and each wished to be
acknowledged the greatest among them.

Spring said: 'I give life, I cause to blossom all the fruits of
the earth.'

Summer said: 'I ripen, I prepare the harvest of all the
fruits of the earth.'

Autumn said: 'I bear forth, I fill the cellars, the granaries,
the barns, with the fruits of the earth.'

Winter said: 'I devour, I consume all the fruits of the
earth, I purge them of vermin and sickness.'

Thus they held forth and argued with violence who was
the greatest among them.

But they forgot that they vaunted only their own power,
and that is lent by God.

So it is between you.

The plaintiff weeps for his loss as if for his birthright, and not a blessing we bestowed on him.

Death boasts of his might, but it comes by us, and he is our servant.

That which you claim does not belong to you.

The power which you vaunt does not come from you.

Yet the quarrel is not without merit. You both have fought well. The one driven by suffering to make his complaint; the other provoked by complaint into telling the truth.

Therefore, plaintiff, to you goes the honour.

And to you, Death, goes the victory.

This is our word and law: each man must give his life to Death, his body to the earth, and his soul to God.


## THE PRAYER OF THE PLOUGHMAN FOR THE SOUL OF HIS WIFE   (Chapter Thirty-Four)

*Here the Ploughman prays for the soul of his wife. The red letter, the great, who shares the name of the plaintiff. This chapter is made in the fashion of a prayer and is the thirty-fourth chapter. And the wife of the Ploughman was thirty-four years old.*


## PLOUGHMAN

Our Father who watches over the whole world for always, God of gods, Lord of lords, who alone workest great marvels, Spirit most powerful, King of kings, the fountain of goodness, Most Holy of holies, both lawgiver and the law, both giver and gift, happy is he who serves You.

Joy and delight of angels, engraver of supreme forms both ancient and newborn, hear me.

O light that shines brightest, light which casts all light on this earth into darkness; light before which all shadows are banished. Light from true light who said in the beginning: 'Let there be light!'

O fire which burns ever without burning out, alpha and omega, beginning and end, hear me.

Salvation and happiness beyond all salvation; true unwavering path to eternal life, the life in which all things live. Truth above all truth, wisdom from which all wisdom flows; You who watch over the just and the unjust.

Healer of all sickness and frailty; who gives to the poor to eat, and comforts the sick; who maintains the harmony of the heavens, who alone knows all human thoughts; sculptor of each human face everchanging; Lord of the heavenly throng, hear me.

Eternal lamp, light eternal, navigator most true, whose ship never founders, bearer of the flag of all victories; founder of hell, who fanned the flames of hell into life; maker of the earthly globe, who holds the wild seas at bay; who stirs the life-giving air; who sets aglow the fire's embers, creator of all elements, of thunder and lightning, of mists and showers, of snow, rain, rainbows, of dew, tempests and frost. Have pity, hear me.

Breath of life of all who draw breath, all those who are gone, all beings eternal, preserver and destroyer; who art that You art, and whom none can know, touch, see, conceive of, or imagine; supreme good above all good, Lord Jesus, receive with mercy the soul of my wife whom I loved.

Grant her eternal rest, bless her with the shower of Your grace, pour upon her the continual dew of Your blessing, guard her safe in the shadow of Your wings. Keep her, take her, Lord, in the fullness of Your embrace, there where the smallest as much as the greatest finds eternal rest; Lord, let her live in Your kingdom, close to angels and archangels, preserve her in eternal happiness.

I ache for Margherita, my truly beloved.

Grant her, gracious Lord, that she may see herself in the mirror of Your almighty and eternal holiness, that she may see herself, and rejoice that she is there in Your bosom where all the choirs of angels sing in Your light.

May all those who count themselves among the flock of

the Shepherd, whosoever they be, come to my aid, that I may say with all strength: 'Amen.'

(Made in the year of grace 1400. The day after the death of my wife Margherita.)